CW01067159

Life in the First Settlement at Sydney Cove

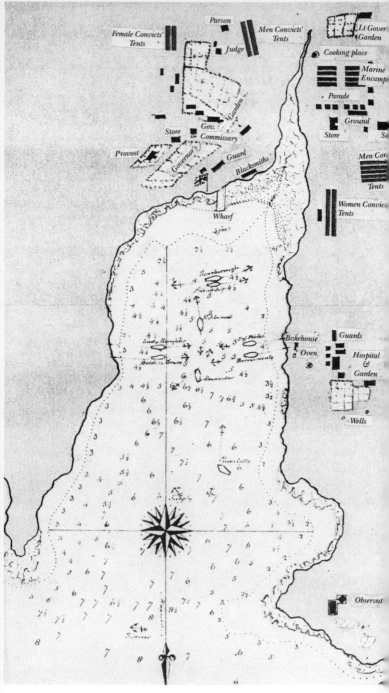

Female Convicts'
Tents

Parson

Men Convicts'
Tents

Lt Gover
Garden

Judge

Cooking place

Marine
Encamp

Parade

Store

Ground

Se

Store

Gov.
Commissary

Garden

Men Co
Tents

Provost

Governor's

Guard

Blacksmiths

Women Convic
Tents

Wharf

Scarborough

Prince of

Fishburn

Golden Grove

Supply

Alexander

Charlotte

Bakehouse
Oven

Guards

Hospital
&
Garden

Wells

Observat

Sydney Cove, Port Jackson.

*The position of the encampment & buildings as they stood 1 March 1788. The
Transports are placed in the Cove as moored on their arrival. Surveyed by
Capt. Hunter.*

Life in
the First Settlement
at Sydney Cove

Bryan Gandevia

Kangaroo Press

Acknowledgments

I wish to thank the following for permission to reproduce illustrations:
The Trustees of the Mitchell and Dixson Libraries, and the Library of New South Wales (cover and page 24)
The National Library of Australia (pages 16 and 17)
The British Museum (Natural History) (pages 26, 27, 28, 29 and 31)

Cover: A Direct North View of Sydney Cove   Thomas Watling, 1794

First published in 1985 by Kangaroo Press Pty Ltd
3 Whitehall Road (PO Box 75) Kenthurst 2154
Typeset by T. & H. Bayfield
Printed in Hong Kong through Bookbuilders Ltd

ISBN 0-86417-038-6

Contents

Contents

Introduction

Two earlier titles in this series — *Growing Up in the First Fleet* and *Growing Up in Phillip's Sydney* — introduced you to the convicts and their guardians who established the first European settlement at Sydney Cove, New South Wales. In this book I shall carry the story a little further by describing how people lived in the settlement's early years. Apart from official reports and accounts, our information about this period comes from the journals of David Collins, the judge-advocate and virtually Governor Phillip's right-hand man, Watkin Tench and Ralph Clark, marine officers, John White, the surgeon-general, and two other doctors (Bowes and Worgan), together with the humble and poorly written notes of a sergeant and a private in the marines. None of these writers was particularly concerned to record his everyday routine, or the everyday chores of anybody else, so that it is necessary to reconstruct their activities from a host of incidental references. Even these become few as the novelty of the new settlement and its surroundings wore off. The new settlers faced the grim realities of isolation and near starvation in an apparently hostile environment and the struggle to survive left little time for writing (if there was any paper to write on). The story I have to tell is the human side of the colony's history, with a little of the essential background in the first and last chapters.

For the important (and less important) events as they occurred, the series of books by John Cobley, *Sydney Cove 1788–1795* (shortly to be extended to 1800) remain indispensable works. I shall give some attention to those aspects of the settlement which influenced health, or the likelihood of disease and death, not only because this is a special interest of mine but also because I should like to show you how health and disease may be influenced by the physical and social environment. Some of these questions were reviewed in more detail in an essay in the *Journal of the Royal Australian Historical Society* in March 1975, 'Socio-medical factors in the evolution of the first settlement at Sydney Cove, 1788–1803'.

And now, try to imagine yourself thousands of kilometres from anywhere, with a few tools and preserved foods, no shops, no houses, no water supply, no toilets, no roads in or out, no electricity, no idea of the climate, and only the clothes you stand up in!

The first weeks

When the First Fleet arrived at Botany Bay in January 1788, the first jobs ashore were to cut fresh grass to feed the sheep and cattle on the ships and to start digging a sawpit to make planks for buildings. Some of the Aborigines were upset to see the ground being cleared and a few big trees chopped down. Other parties went fishing with lines and nets to obtain much needed fresh food after the long voyage. Still other groups explored the area around the bay to find a suitable area for the new settlement. Surgeon Bowes, wandering alone, got himself lost in the unfamiliar Australian bush but luckily found his way back to the shore. The marines provided guards for all these activities, and even this tedious task must have been a relief after six months on tiny ships.

Phillip was not happy with the Botany Bay area. It was not a very safe anchorage for his ships and there was little fresh running water. He also thought that it might be unhealthy; the mangrove swamps reminded him of the West Indies, where mangroves were associated with frightening outbreaks of serious fevers. He and some of his officers and men rowed to Port Jackson where Phillip had no difficulty in selecting Sydney Cove as the site for the first permanent settlement in Australia.

So just as the sawpit was finished (it had been difficult to dig and shore up in the sandy soil) orders came to dismantle it. It was the first of many frustrating and unrewarding tasks to be undertaken by the new Australians. The fleet then sailed around to what we usually call Sydney Harbour.

In Sydney Cove the work of disembarkation

Entrance of Port Jackson 27 January 1788   William Bradley

Sydney Cove, Port Jackson 1788   William Bradley

began all over again. At first the convicts were landed daily and returned to the ships for their midday dinner and again in the evening. Within a fortnight all the marines and convicts had been landed. The women convicts were sent ashore last. This event led to a wild party on a hot, stormy night punctuated by frightening thunder, lightning and rain; convicts from Britain were not used to such semi-tropical storms. Perhaps the storm was an omen of the future, for it was the last big party the convicts were to enjoy. On the following morning there was a formal parade of the whole population — officials, marines and convicts — at which Phillip was proclaimed as governor and the settlement was officially established. The governor addressed the convicts on the need for all to work together for the common good; discipline would be strict but fair.

Finding Shelter

Tents provided most of the shelter in these early days. The first building to be erected was the governor's timber and canvas house which had been made up in England. This leaky hut had to serve until a two-storeyed house, made of local bricks, was built over the next few months. It was the only house in the colony to have glass windows for some years. Other urgent constructions were a wharf, a safe storehouse to preserve the provisions on which the settlement's survival depended, a guardhouse, a magazine for gunpowder and a cellar for the spirits. A hospital was built of wood, with a shingle roof, and was immediately filled with patients.

Barracks for the marines were begun but by the time winter came only a few officers had even the simple mud-plastered huts made of split logs and sawn timber which were the first homes. These were kept low to save timber. The settlers found that the logs from the eucalypts did not split easily, and were surprised that some of the wood did not float. The houses had a roof thatched with reeds or grass (later wooden shingles were made from the she-oak or casuarina tree). Sliding windows were made of sticks, and the doors swung on leather hinges. The floors were earth and the fireplaces were made of mud and stone until bricks were available. The bricks came from clay soil near the present Central railway station, but they did not solve all the building problems because there was not enough lime to make good mortar. The bricks had to be set in mud or clay, and so it was not surprising that many chimneys, and even the partly built walls of the governor's house, collapsed in heavy rain. It was probably a year or more before everyone had some reasonable shelter, but even then one convict was happy to have a large hollow log to himself.

Once the essential buildings were under way, there were complaints about the building program. Major Ross, the commanding officer of the marines, wanted some forts, and the Reverend Johnson was unhappy that there was no plan to build a church. But Phillip was wise enough to see that the risks to his settlement were greater from within it than from the ships of a foreign power such as France, or from the Aborigines. Although he was strict about attendance at church services, these could be held in the open air or any available building, and a church was a luxury which he could not afford.

Food and Water

At least as important as shelter was food. At first the weekly ration was 7 lb (just over 3 kg) of bread or flour and the same of salt beef (or else 4 lb [almost 2 kg] of salt pork), three pints (about 1.7 l) of dried peas, 6 oz (170 g) of butter (for the short time it lasted) and either ½ lb (250 g) rice or some extra flour. Nothing else was available, except for a daily issue of rum to the marines (which did not last long either) and a smaller issue to their wives, for the sake of their health it was said. Fish were sometimes available but the catch was rarely enough for 200 people for one day, usually much less. The women received two-thirds of the male ration, and so did children over the age of ten (children of 13 or so were probably regarded as adults). Under two years of age the children were given a quarter ration, and a half between two and ten years. Everyone did his or her own cooking. It is hard to imagine cooking and eating this monotonous food every day, especially on an open fire or hearth and with a desperate shortage of cooking utensils — the convicts had only wooden bowls!

What was worse, the quality of these foods was poor. The meat had been salted in barrels years before, and weevils, maggots and rats enjoyed the rice and flour. Some of the provisions were declared unfit to eat — perhaps a happy benefit to the few pigs and dogs in the settlement! One officer described how he held the meat over the fire and caught the drips on a plate so as to preserve as much as possible; if boiled the meat simply seemed to disappear.

Because Phillip had made sure the convicts got fresh food at the ports of call on the voyage out, the First Fleet had not suffered much from scurvy. Scurvy is a disease caused by lack of vitamin C found in oranges and lemons in good quantity, and in lesser amounts in many other fresh vegetables and fruits. The symptoms include sore mouth and throat, skin and joint troubles, and a tendency to bleeding; if untreated, sufferers eventually die. Scurvy now began to appear in the settlement, and even the governor did not escape. He and his doctors knew that fresh foods were urgently needed. Within days of their arrival gardens were established near the governor's house and near the hospital. These seemed 'luxuriant' in a couple of weeks but in general the plants and seedlings did not do well. Fortunately, local forms of celery, spinach, parsley and other edible plants were quite plentiful nearby, and a form of tea was made from the native sarsaparilla. Unfortunately, the native currant, which is rich in vitamin C, was not so common. Convicts and convalescent patients were sent out to collect 'greens', as they were called. These parties sometimes had a marine guard, especially after one convict was 'Barberasely Killed' while he 'ware a-going for greens' (Private Easty was not good at spelling). This unhappy incident was a sign of the increasing tension between the two races, probably because the Aborigines were provoked by the behaviour of undisciplined convicts. The convicts were not strictly confined, and were able to wander within certain limits close to the settlement.

Within a month of arrival, there was concern that the little stream that provided water was drying up. The settlers found that it arose only from some marshes near Hyde Park and out towards Botany Bay. The little creek became known as the Tank Stream after Phillip had dug large tanks in its course to help preserve the water. It now runs underground close to George Street. The first conservation order in Australia was one to preserve the trees along its banks.

The limited supply of water, perhaps polluted from the camp, probably aggravated the outbreak of dysentery which affected the marines and their officers as well as the convicts. In those days, this severe form of diarrhoea usually appeared in new or temporary camps because not enough was known about personal and public hygiene (handwashing and the proper disposal of nightsoil, for example). About two hundred people, or one in five, were in need of treatment by March and about fifty died from this and other causes. With the coming of winter the epidemic died away; there were probably fewer flies to help spread infection. All medicines were in very short supply, so it was lucky that the surgeons found the gum from some of the native trees helpful. The hospital was overcrowded and very primitive, and there were no trained nurses. Some convicts were allotted to help look after the sick. Lieutenant Clark took one of the sick officers into his tent to help look after him.

Yellow Gum Plant

Settling down

It was difficult for both convicts and marines to adjust themselves to this strange new way of life, especially for the convicts who mostly came from city slums. There were fights, thefts and attempted escapes, and men broke the rules about mixing with the women and bartering rum. There were many court sittings, with the marine officers acting as judges (there were no juries), many floggings and a few hangings. Although Phillip tried to be lenient and reduced many of the sentences, he was criticised for punishing the marines more severely than the convicts. He probably did this to enforce discipline; he had to rely absolutely on the marines to keep order amongst convicts who outnumbered them by almost three to one. The officers were not setting a good example. They were constantly arguing among themselves and on the advice of Major Ross they refused to supervise the daily work of the convicts. Phillip had to appoint overseers from amongst the convicts themselves, an arrangement which was not satisfactory because few of them had the necessary personal qualities or skills.

15

The seamen from the ships were also a nuisance, especially by trading in rum with the convicts, who offered native animals or Aboriginal artefacts for exchange. They were occupied in preparing their ships as best they could for the return voyage. They had to load water from the stream or wells into wooden barrels and to take on wood for fires. Phillip allowed them to chop down trees but insisted that they must grub out the stumps. Probably they also sent parties out to collect whatever 'greens' they could find. Ships' carpenters from the *Sirius* and *Supply* helped to make small rowing boats for the settlement's use. Most of the ships had departed by the middle of the year (1788).

Phillip established two subsidiary settlements during 1788. The first, at Norfolk Island,

Brickfield Hill and Village on the High Road to Parramatta

consisted of Lieutenant P.G. King as commander, with a surgeon, several seamen and marines, and fifteen convicts, including six women. It was established mainly to forestall the French, because the British thought flax and timber from the Norfolk Island pines would be suitable for naval use. The second settlement, at Rose Hill, (Parramatta), was established in November because the soil was better for cultivation and the country was less wooded than near Sydney Cove.

It was high time that the colony settled down. In many ways it did, and most of the convicts behaved better than was expected. Let us turn now to look at the kind of life and the everyday activities of the thousand or so people who were to be almost completely isolated from the outside world for over two years.

Edward Dayes (after Watling)

The people of Sydney Cove

At the head of the new colony was Governor Arthur Phillip, aged 50 years. His father, who taught languages, came from Frankfurt, and the family was not well off. Phillip had been educated for the navy from the age of thirteen. After service in many parts of the world with the British and Portuguese navies he was retired on half pay and was a farmer at the time of his appointment. After his return from New South Wales he lived in retirement at Bath until his death in 1814. Lieutenant Philip Gidley King (1758–1808) was the governor's aide-de-camp, but he was sent to establish the settlement on Norfolk Island early in 1788.

The most important member of Phillip's staff was David Collins, aged 32, a captain in the marines who had seen active service in North America, and the son of a marine officer. Although he had no legal training, he was appointed judge-advocate, supervising the administration of justice. He was the chief recorder of events in the colony from its beginning until he left in 1796. He later became governor of Tasmania, dying suddenly in Hobart in 1810.

There were four surgeons, the senior being John White (1756–1832). He entered the navy as a surgeon's mate in 1778, and served in the Indian and West Indian areas, becoming a skilled and experienced surgeon. He became irritable and depressed after the publication in 1790 of his important book on the voyage to New South Wales, the early months of the settlement and the local flora and fauna. Perhaps because of his ill temper, he unfortunately did not publish the promised continuation volume. Although he was apparently difficult to get on with, he and his fellow surgeons did as much as they could in difficult circumstances to preserve health and treat the sick. White remained in the colony until December 1794.

The Rev. Richard Johnson B.A.

The Reverend Richard Johnson, although 35 years of age, was a relatively inexperienced curate with rather rigid religious views. He was the only senior member of the expedition to be allowed to bring his wife. He found his missionary work among the convicts unrewarding but his ability as a gardener was invaluable to the colony. Johnson returned to England, rather disillusioned, in 1800. Other officials included a surveyor and a stores officer.

Major Robert Ross, commandant of the battalion of marines, was then aged nearly 50 years. He joined the marines in 1756, fought in the wars in North America, and saw active service in Mediterranean and West Indian waters. Uniformly disliked himself, he hated the country and he must have spent a rather lonely time with his young son, John, as his chief company. Phillip sent him to take charge of Norfolk Island in 1790 when he decided to send King to England to describe the problems of the settlement personally to the authorities.

Captain Watkin Tench

Of the other officers, the most interesting was the well-educated Captain Watkin Tench (1758–1833), the son of a schoolmaster. Tench wrote the most readable and human account of the colony's first few years; in addition to a sense of duty he had a sense of humour. Three other marines kept journals: Lieutenant Ralph Clark, who was sorry for himself a lot of the time, and Sergeant Scott and Private Easty who, like good soldiers, were apparently resigned to whatever might happen. Some 27 wives and 11 children accompanied the marines, of whom there were nearly two hundred.

Two naval vessels, the *Sirius* and the *Supply*, accompanied six convict transports and three storeships, altogether manned by over 400 seamen. The senior naval officer, after Phillip, was Captain John Hunter (1737–1821), who had worked his way up in rank, like King, from the lowly position of captain's servant. He had served in many parts of the world and was an expert navigator. He later became governor of New South Wales. Hunter, Lieutenant Bradley and King were the chief naval officers to keep journals.

Finally, there were the convicts, about 750 of them, including 190 or so women with a dozen children. Most had been sentenced to seven years' imprisonment; some unfortunates had only a year or two of their sentences yet to run. Fifteen were over 50 years of age (one was 80) and there were seven aged between 10 and 15 years; the great majority of both sexes were aged 20 to 35 years. Stealing in one way or another was by far the commonest crime, but most of the convicts were professional thieves. The crimes seem petty by today's standards but the value of the articles stolen was frequently reduced so as to avoid an obligatory death sentence. Most of the convicts came from the poorest and most underprivileged sections of British society, whether from city slums or rural areas. The Irish, mostly peasants living in gross poverty and understandably disliking their English masters, were different in some ways, but they began to arrive only late in the period with which we are mainly concerned. Collectively, the convicts had little or no education, and their experience of life was such that it would not be easy for them to adapt to the very different way of life awaiting them in New South Wales.

All these people, with their European customs and culture, were deposited on the very edge of a remote and unfriendly land. A strange land, where the trees lost their bark and not their leaves in the spring, and where many other things were topsy-turvy. And in it there was a race of native people, who were sometimes friendly, sometimes hostile, and who seemed to think that anything and everything belonged to everyone or anyone. Later in this book we shall look briefly at these original inhabitants, the Aborigines, and their problems produced by this cultural clash. These problems were quite different from the problems that faced the European settlers, and they really deserve a book on their own.

Now that we have met the main characters, let us look more closely at each of the social groups. We shall begin with the marines because they show us how the community was organised. They provide a good background against which we can more clearly follow the life styles of the higher and the lower social orders. The Aborigines, of course, stand by themselves.

The marines and their families

A working life

The first sign of order in the colony was the reassuring issue of the 'orders of the day' for the detachment of Royal Marines, commanded by Major Robert Ross. The orders set out a password for the day, and named a captain as the day's duty officer, one or two lieutenants to take charge of the guards and one or two more to be available if required. This work could be demanding; Ralph Clark had to sleep in his clothes two nights in a row. Guards were set at important points, such as the governor's house, the stores, the hospital, the landing area and the fishery established at Botany Bay. Patrols were established to catch stragglers from the camp's rough boundaries. When the colony was becoming anxious about the lack of further ships from England, Captain Hunter suggested a flagstaff and a lookout at South Head, and these were duly established by Hunter himself. Later it became the responsibility of yet another marine detachment to man the outpost. By the end of 1788, a permanent detachment was also required at Rose Hill (Parramatta). Small detachments accompanied the governor and other officers on their several expeditions outside the settlement.

Life was governed by the beat of drums; there were 12 drummers to take turns. They signalled 'Revallie' at sunrise, midday dinner time and lights out around 9 p.m., as well as the Sunday church parade. No one, including wives, was to be absent from church 'on any account whatever', and the troops were to be in their full uniform, so unsuited to the hot climate. Although Major Ross and his officers would not supervise the convicts

English officer and lady in New Holland
Malaspina Expedition Drawings, 1793

at work, they did make sure that for Divine
Service the convicts were 'as clean as
circumstances will admit of'. The marines' lines
(tent area) were to be kept clean and tidy. The tent
flaps were to be left open, weather permitting, to
allow plenty of fresh air, one of the few hygiene
measures possible in those days. Roll calls were to
be made twice daily. Much of this formality
disappeared over the months. No soldierly
training activities were undertaken, and parades
were held only on special occasions.

Whatever their duties were, both officers and
men believed that they were doing work not
normally expected of a marine battalion. To some
extent this was true, and Phillip supported the
officers when they asked for an extra pay
allowance. According to Private Easty's diary, the
marines 'Turned out and Said that they Could not
work aney longer with out being Paid for itt'. Only
the day before this Major Ross had placed several
of his officers under arrest over a technical matter
of no great importance. We may conclude that
morale amongst the marines could not have been
high. Indeed, one convict wrote that the marines

were not content with seeing those who lived better even though they also saw 'us who lived worse'.

The marines were of course fully employed in helping to build their own barracks and other buildings. They cut down trees, and worked in the sawpit, at the quarry and in the blacksmith's shop. Many of them no doubt tried gardening. Sergeant Scott, a family man, was proud of getting sixteen chickens from eighteen eggs, and annoyed when two died, one drowned and eleven were taken by 'An Anamel'. He got his revenge when he trapped the rat, which the family probably ate. He and his wife must often have recalled their Christmas dinner on board ship in 1787:

> Dinned off a piece of pork & apple Sauce and a pice of Beef & plum pudding, and Crowned the Day With 4 Bottles of Rum, Which Was the Best We Vitr'ens [veterans] Could Afford.

However they managed it, the marines must have lived better than the convicts because their death rate over the first five years of the settlement was much lower than that of the convicts.

Only when they got into trouble, which they often did, do we learn anything more of their off-duty activities. One convict lost seven pairs of trousers, four shirts and two pairs of shoes playing cards with one or two of the marines. Private Easty records his own sin thus: 'this Night about 1/2 past 8 oclock I was confined by Serjt. Hume for bringing a feamale Convict into Camp'. He was tried and found guilty and a few days later he wrote 'Easty & Clayton received 150 Laches Each'. Easty was a sensitive man and we often feel his sympathy when he records the death of one of his friends ('Lift a Wife and 2 small Children', for example). There was some *esprit de corps* in the battalion, for when six marines were hanged for regularly stealing from the small stock of provisions Easty remarked that 'there was hardly a marine present but what Shed tears offacers and men'. Phillip obviously made an example of these men; they had obtained duplicate keys to

View of the East Side of Sydney Cove, Port Jackson from the

the locks on the store, and whenever one of them was the sentinel on the store his colleagues would plunder it with little risk of interruption.

Wives and families

Very little is recorded about the 27 wives of the marines and their 36 or so children who arrived on the First Fleet. The mothers had to keep a close eye on their children; there were no fences and it is surprising that none of them seem to have got lost in the surrounding bush. Keeping house was difficult. There was an open fire to keep alight, water to cart and perhaps some chickens and a pig or a goat to look after. And how to cook an occasional piece of emu or kangaroo, the fruit of

Anchorage. The Governors House.   George Raper

the cabbage tree and other strange vegetables, not to mention the odd crow, parrot or dog? Without cupboards, a marine's wife would have to keep her few provisions away from the rats and the pigs which roamed freely around the camp. She would have to learn that meat became flyblown within hours, no matter how careful she was. Sergeant Scott's journal seems to suggest that the marine families formed small social groups amongst themselves; it is unlikely that the children were allowed to play with the convict children. Perhaps this 'togetherness' is shown in the case of Sergeant Harmsworth's wife, who lost her husband and one child from fever. She was befriended by Corporal Standfield whom she later married. None of the marines married convict women, although some long-lasting liaisons were formed.

The governor and the gentlemen

Governor Phillip

The governor's days must have been crowded. We have no notes of Phillip's daily routine except when he went on excursions to the west and north, to Rose Hill, Broken Bay or the Hawkesbury River near Windsor. A settlement was soon formed at Parramatta where the ground was more easily cleared and the soil was better for cultivation. As Phillip had to spend some time there another tiny Government House was built (some remains of this building can still be seen at Old Government House). His concern for his people must have required regular inspections to understand their problems and to see progress. For example, he visited the hospital and indicated his concern for the pitiable state of the patients,

The Melancholy Loss of HMS *Sirius*, Wrecked on Norfolk Island.

for whom the surgeons could provide little in the way of comforts or little luxuries. He read the proceedings of the many trials and confirmed or reduced the sentences. Much of his time was taken up listening to complaints and trying to settle arguments among his staff and marine officers. Before the departure of any ship for England there was great activity in preparing despatches and writing letters to the authorities and to friends 'at home'.

Above all, the governor had to take responsibility, alone, for many difficult decisions affecting the welfare, and even the survival, of the settlement. He had to distribute the convicts to best advantage between Sydney Cove, Parramatta and Norfolk Island. The first tiny settlement on Norfolk Island was later expanded because its fertile soil allowed it to become more nearly self-supporting than the mainland colony. Phillip was obliged to send the *Sirius*, under Captain Hunter, to the Cape of Good Hope for supplies (chiefly flour as this was the best the ship could manage). Between October 1788 and May 1789 Hunter did this by going right around the world. After the *Sirius* was wrecked off Norfolk Island in March 1790, Phillip had to send his only remaining ship,

George Raper

the little *Supply*, to Batavia for supplies. This left the colony in complete isolation, but if the ship were not sent, or if it failed to return, the settlement inevitably faced starvation. No lives were lost with the *Sirius*, but the departure of the ship they knew so well caused no little sadness and some understandable alarm.

Some of Phillip's most difficult decisions were concerned with the rationing of the food supplies. From late in 1789 to mid-1790 and again in mid-1791 the stores were sufficient for only a few weeks. At the worst period, Phillip had to reduce the weekly ration to 2 lb (nearly 1 kg) salt pork, 2½ lb flour and 2 lb rice (full of weevils) or some dried peas. This ration provides insufficient calories for all but light work, and it lacks vitamin C as well as vitamins of the B group. Lack of the latter may cause troubles with the function of the heart and the nervous system. There is evidence of these troubles in the settlement at this time, although no real medical records survive. To his great credit, Phillip made no distinction between the free people and the convicts. He took the same rations himself and gave to the general store his private supplies which he had brought from England.

Not all the governor's decisions were popular with his officers, who sometimes criticised him. Nonetheless, he did his best to maintain good relations among them all. He would occasionally ask some of the officers to breakfast or dinner with him, although in the bad days they had to bring their own bread! He was host to more formal parties on formal occasions such as royal birthdays. The first of these, after Phillip's installation ceremony, was rather spoilt by maggots in the mutton killed only the day before — the effects of the warm Australian climate and the numerous flies had still to be learnt.

Phillip knew that good leadership is best achieved by example. He showed personal courage in going alone and unarmed to greet possibly hostile natives. In this way, at Manly Cove one day, he received a spear wound near the shoulder from which he was lucky to recover.

Indeed, with nearly 4 metres of spear sticking out in front of him, and almost 8 centimetres out the back of his shoulder, he was lucky to escape at all. Fortunately, Lieutenant Waterhouse managed to break the spear off, and the governor staggered to his boat. Surgeon Balmain inspected the wound and predicted that it would not be fatal. Balmain removed the spear and Phillip, although suffering from scurvy, was active again within a fortnight. Had the spear entered a few centimeters lower it would have punctured the lung, almost certainly leading to death from infection in those pre-antibiotic days. To show that he wanted friendly relationships Phillip did not seek revenge.

The officers

Except for the even-tempered Collins, who lived with the governor, the other officers showed the stresses and strains of isolation and hunger by frequently quarrelling. Two of the surgeons fought a duel with pistols after a dinner with the governor, who was called out to calm them down. Unlike Phillip, who was always optimistic, most of the officers became disillusioned with the settlement and its prospects.

During the early months the officers and their marine servants spent as much time as they could bringing in timber, especially cabbage trees, from all around the harbour to build their huts. The officers even had to collect their own rushes for thatching — hence the name of Rushcutters Bay.

The Hunted Rushcutter   Banks MS

The chaplain spent a hard day or so gathering grass for the same purpose or perhaps for animal feed. The officers' work for the settlement was divided between guard duty and hearing court cases. All, including the chaplain, took turns at supervising the fishing boats at night to prevent the catch from being stolen.

In their spare time the officers could go fishing, but the sharks were quick to take their hooks and lines. One fishing party collected young midshipman Ferguson from the lookout at South Head to return to Sydney Cove. A whale upset the boat and Ferguson and two marines were drowned. Hunting was popular, generally on foot and for birds. Phillip's greyhound ran down a kangaroo on one occasion but usually kangaroos were not easily caught or shot. Any fresh food, such as turtle from Lord Howe Island, or an emu shot by good chance, was often an excuse for a small party. One of the surgeons 'dined most heartily ... on a fine dog, and [I] hope I shall again have an invitation to a similar repast'. Some officers, like Tench and surgeon Worgan, enjoyed exploring the countryside, especially with 'a bottle of O be joyful' (rum or wine) to go with lunch. These excursions were often quite eventful. Once Tench got stuck in mud near Botany Bay, and once some of the party became very ill after eating native berries. It was hard work walking through dense trackless scrub, clambering over large rocks and wading streams; their shoes and clothes soon suffered. When food supplies ran low, these expeditions were too much for their strength.

The influence of Sir Joseph Banks in London encouraged people to collect strange new plants to send home for scientific study. The surgeons White and Considen were active in these tasks, while surgeon Bowes was specially interested in collecting insects and birds. White took special note of the birds and animals he saw. He and Bowes, like several of the naval officers, could draw but White later seems to have preferred to supervise the convict artist, Thomas Watling, in drawing his specimens. William Dawes set up his observatory at what is now Dawes Point and spent

'1 Kanguroo Rat 2 A Young ditto 3 Jaws of ditto' from Phillip's journal showing his keen interest in natural history

many evenings looking at the stars. Collins took a daily walk to a point where he could see the flagstaff at the lookout station, often with one or two friends.

From necessity much time was spent in gardening. Phillip had no authority to make land grants to the officers, much to their disappointment, but they were allotted garden plots. 'Parade duties and show' were forgotten, and spades and hoes were carried instead of muskets. A barrow was a prized possession. The governor's garden flourished only temporarily in the sandy soil near Farm Cove. What is now Garden Island was given over to the men of the *Sirius* for a garden and to hold the livestock belonging to the ship's officers. The best gardens were those of Major Ross and the Reverend Richard Johnson, whose house was in Bridge Street. Indeed, the chaplain was acknowledged as the best gardener in the colony. By giving vegetables to the hospital, he probably saved more lives than the surgeons. A major difficulty was the lack of animal manure; one wonders if the secret of the chaplain's success was to use human manure.

Of games and sporting activities we have no information, but between them all the officers and gentlemen probably had quite a range of books. Worgan's friends may have enjoyed a sing-song around the piano which he brought with him on the *Sirus*. Later, the British government sent a supply of port wine and tobacco which might have added a little to such occasions. Much later, picnics around the harbour, with fresh oysters off the rocks, were popular, especially with the ladies, but in the early days there were no officers' wives. Phillip did not bring his wife, and perhaps for this reason Lieutenant Ralph Clark was not allowed to bring his young wife and child, but every Sunday he kissed her portrait, at least for some months.

The convict men

In his speech to the convicts after his commission
had been read at a formal ceremony and parade
in February 1788, Governor Phillip warned the
convicts that they would be treated strictly but
fairly. He told them they would have to work but
no harder than on an English farm. They were to
behave, particularly in not stealing the vital
provisions and the livestock (sheep, pigs, goats
and cattle) needed for breeding. Phillip knew that
he could not suddenly expect these unfortunate
people, mostly professional criminals from city
slums, to reform themselves. The chaplain tried
very hard to reform them, visiting them in their
huts and at the hospital. In his Sunday sermons he
preached vigorously on the terrible hell waiting
for sinners and of God's forgiveness to those who
changed their wicked ways. Sadly, he eventually
admitted his failure to gather many genuine
converts. Nonetheless, except for some persistent
offenders, the First Fleet convicts came to behave
quite well; an elite group did not mix with the
worst elements of convict society, and convict
overseers of work gangs were drawn from it.
By 1792, it was noticed that the troublemakers
came mostly from among the later arrivals.

Only once, in December 1791, was Phillip faced
with a minor revolt, or what today we would call a
demonstration. The convicts were objecting to
the issue of their rations daily instead of weekly.
This change was necessary because the convicts
were eating their week's ration in a couple of days;
being hungry, they were then inclined to steal to
feed themselves for the rest of the week. Phillip
confronted the mob, declined their request and
explained the reasons. He threatened to deal
severely with the ringleaders in any further
disturbance. It is reported that he then received

the support and agreement of the assembled convicts. The incident reflects the quality of Phillip's leadership.

Many lapses from good behaviour are revealed in the court records and these incidentally give us some insight into everyday events. The chief crimes were precisely those which Phillip had predicted, and understandably so, in the 'hungry years' from 1789. Thefts from houses, stores or gardens were mostly for food, sometimes for clothing and occasionally for liquor. Assaults, killings and other desperate crimes were not common. No one was secure from robbery, including the governor and the chaplain (who, rather later, slept with pistols under his pillow!).

At work

The convicts did work, although they never achieved as much as their guardians wished or thought possible. Phillip realised that most of them were unaccustomed to farm labour, and he understood that they could do little physical work when they had so little to eat. However, when he reduced the working hours (to from sunrise to 1 p.m. or from 5 to 9 a.m. and 4 to 4.30 p.m.) to allow the convicts more time in their own gardens he found that this gave them more time to get into trouble. At this stage, each convict was ordered only 'to do as much work as his strength would permit'. Sometimes the convict was given task work, that is, a certain amount of work to be done in the day, after which he was free to do as he liked. Although intended as an incentive, it made for hasty and badly done work; a lot of new chimneys fell down in the rain as a result of this approach.

About a quarter of the convicts were employed in growing food. There were no ploughs and no working animals. The land was cleared, the stumps grubbed out and burned, the ground hoed and the seed sown all by hand. One poor fellow ate the bean seeds he had been sent to plant. Most of the rest of the labour force worked

A convict's view of life   Edward Lilburn, c. 1840

on public buildings, in making bricks, sawing
wood and splitting shingles, constructing rough
roads, digging wells and rolling logs to form a
bridge over the Tank Stream. Many, at the worst
period about 20 per cent, were too old or too sick
for any such heavy work.

During the voyage out Phillip had taken note of
those convicts who were tradesmen or had special
skills. There were too few carpenters and too few
farmers, but he did find one or two bakers and
bricklayers, thatchers, a shoemaker, blacksmith,
wheelwright, locksmith, candlemaker, cooper,
and even a surgeon and a barber or two to work in
the hospital. All these men were put to their
appropriate tasks and were usually made
supervisors with the responsibility to teach
others. Some, probably the less fit, had to cut
rushes or gather greens. A trusted few were given
arms and employed as hunters, but they seem to
have found the kangaroos more difficult to shoot
than English game. One unfortunate man lost the
few cows in the colony when he left them
unattended while he went off for his dinner. This
was a serious loss; a herd of descendants was
located at the Cowpastures about seven years
later. Some trusted convicts, at their own
suggestion, formed a 'police watch' which
patrolled the settlement at night to prevent
robberies. Their other duty was to make sure that
everyone attended church parade on Sundays.

Clothes

Despite a special issue before disembarking, clothing was to become a major problem. Almost all the clothes were worn out by 1790. The frocks (loose shirts) and trousers were of such light material that they wore out in a fortnight. A heavier material (duck, like denim) was sent out to be made up locally by the women but much of it suffered water damage on the ship. Shoes seem to have been issued less than once a year, and even when kangaroo skin could be tanned it was unsuitable for soles. By 1790, even the marine guard was parading in bare feet, and a surgeon had to borrow shoes and clothing from his colleagues. One pair of yarn stockings issued at one stage could scarcely have served for a year or two. The need for self-reliance and repairs is reflected in the fact that everyone received an issue of needles and thread. Fortunately, many of the convicts brought out a chest containing what private possessions they had. It is clear from the records that these sometimes included quite substantial amounts of clothing. The shortage led to many thefts and arguments over ownership, and it became necessary to order that clothing must not be sold or bartered. There were some skilled tailors in the work force but their work was probably limited to commissions from the officers who had brought out their own materials. Lieutenant Clark employed expert women convicts to make him gloves and nightcaps before the ships left England, so the making and repair of garments offered some of the convicts gainful work in their spare time.

Bedding and blankets for the convicts were insufficient on arrival and there seems to be no reference to any government issue in the first years after their arrival. Grass and rushes must have made the convicts' mattresses.

Punishment

Punishment was an ever-present threat to the convicts, although it was only a little less remote for the marines. Flogging was common, usually of 50 lashes or so, but more for serious offences. These floggings were less severe than in the army or navy of those days. Flogging was ordered not only as a punishment to the offender but also because it was believed to deter others from committing similar misdeeds. It did not work in this way and it was said of some of the convicts that they feared punishment less than they feared work. There were several executions for such crimes as robbing the stores. A few convicts were confined for a week or so on Pinchgut Island on bread and water. Rations were reduced as a punishment for failing to attend church. Convicts who tried to escape from the isolated settlement were certain to fail because of its isolation, the lack of food in the bush and the risk of being killed by the natives. Nonetheless, such attempts were severely punished if the escapee was caught. Sometimes convicts were made to wear a canvas 'R' or 'T' (for 'rogue' or 'thief') stitched to their clothing. Legirons were rarely used.

Despite the many punishments, the fairness and justice which Phillip promised did exist, at least to judge by the number of acquittals in the numerous court cases. Sometimes it was a 'rough justice'. Some convicts employed at the hospital were acquitted for lack of proof of stealing eighteen bottles of wine used in the treatment of the sick. However, as suspicion was very high, they were taken away from their easy jobs and put to work in the fields! On the other hand, Anthony Rope, accused of stealing a goat, told the unlikely story that he had found it lying on a rock with its skin 'worried' as if by a wild animal. He was found not guilty but it is curious that he should have found the goat on the eve of his marriage to Mary Pulley. A pie made of fresh meat was served at the wedding party!

Escape

The idea of escape must often have occurred to the convicts. Some walked to Botany Bay in the hope of obtaining a passage back to Europe in the French ships waiting there, but La Perouse sent them back. One convict was found hidden in the hold of one of the returning British transports, and others were suspected of escaping in this way. Phillip feared that the masters of these ships would be glad to obtain the services of the best of his convicts. One remarkable group, led by William Bryant, a fisherman, stole a boat and made their way to the Dutch settlement in Timor. The party, which included Bryant's wife and two children, were eventually handed over to a visiting British ship and the survivors returned to England.

Escape by land was impossible in the early years. Those who attempted it died of starvation or were killed by the natives (who unaccountably helped other lost convicts); a few returned half-starved to the settlement. The Irish peasants thought that they could walk to China a hundred or so kilometres away, while others believed in a town not too far away to the north. Phillip remarked that this idea was 'an evil which will cure itself'!

Entertainment

The convicts occasionally had parties at which singing sometimes went on for long after lights (and fires) out at 8.45 p.m. Gambling at cards was a popular vice; two men were caught playing as late as 2 a.m. They also enjoyed bathing at the beaches although probably few of them could swim.

A game called cross sticks would cause a crowd to gather and become very excited and noisy. The game has not been identified, but it might have been a contest between two men with long wooden sticks as weapons. Perhaps it was a less exciting game depending on how far one could hit one stick with another. Some convicts spent their spare time collecting animals, birds, gum and greens for sale or exchange with the sailors on the ships. Once they put on a play which was attended by the governor and all the officers. Although it was apparently a success, no other similar entertainment seems to have been attempted. There were huge bonfires and a little grog on the King's Birthday in June 1788. Perhaps the convict who gave his occupation as conjurer did some tricks for his friends, and perhaps the fortune-teller had some idle customers. Very few of the convicts could read but there was little to read except the clergyman's religious tracts.

The expirees

Phillip was faced with the problem of what to do with those convicts whose sentences had expired. He decided that they should continue to work for their rations, more or less as before. As an experiment, he granted land to one James Ruse, and this was the beginning of Experiment Farm. Phillip took a deliberate risk because there were many who said the land was too poor to support anyone. Fortunately for Phillip, Ruse was successful, at least in the first years, and his success was a stimulus to the officers when they were allowed to take up land for farming. The convicts to whom Phillip granted pardons were usually those who had worked well in a specialist job. They continued in the same work as free men. The first of the emancipists, as they were called, were the man who organised the brickworks and a surgeon who had assisted in the hospital. The emancipists were to grow in numbers, in economic importance and in political influence, but that is a much later story.

The convict women

The female convicts, numbering about 180, acquired a reputation for behaving very badly and being difficult to control. They could use very bad language; they did not follow the moral standards expected of them (but not of the men); and they could fight very well. However, as with the men, these criticisms applied mainly to an incorrigible minority. Some ingenious and degrading punishments were devised for this group, but without much effect. As an example to all, one had her hair shaved off and had to wear a canvas frock with 'RS' (receiver of stolen goods) on it in large letters. Women were sometimes flogged and occasionally forced to wear an iron collar. They could also be made to do manual work like the men. One infamous female was hanged for stealing clothing: she died 'generally reviled and unpitied' even by the other convicts, indeed a saddening thought. That they were not all such hardened characters is shown by the fact that many of them were seen to be in tears during one of the Reverend Johnson's sermons.

Clothes

When the women stepped ashore from the transports, all were clean and neat, and some had saved their best clothes for the occasion. The seamen were said to have bought them clothes at the ports en route. Indeed, Ann Smith was so disgusted with the clothing issued before disembarking that she threw it on the deck and refused it all. But the issue clothing for women was not only flimsy but also in even shorter supply than the men's because much of it had been left in England by mistake. Within a year or two the shortage was desperate and, according to one observer, much ingenuity was used in patching, substituting and improvising to 'eke out wretchedness, and preserve the remains of decency'. Many of the women were formerly employed as milliners, or lace makers, although most whose occupation is known were servants. Even by 1792 the issue of clothing was not generous: each woman received a cloth petticoat, a coarse shift, pair of shoes, pair of yarn stockings, pins, needles, thread, scissors and a thimble — surely an indication that the government expected them to be industrious seamstresses! They did of course do much work of this kind, as well as laundry, for all classes of men in the settlement in return for tobacco, money, food or other little luxuries, including illegal spirits. When cloth was available, they made shirts for the men and later some of their own clothes.

At work

Phillip considered that women were not capable of heavy work and that those who had children were fully occupied in looking after them. Some of the others were set to work collecting shells (these were burnt to make lime for mortar), making wooden pegs to keep shingles in position, and collecting grass. They probably also collected oysters and greens from close to the settlement, and they would as a rule have had to fetch and carry their own wood and water. No doubt the wives and mothers in particular would have helped in the gardens if they could share in the produce. Very few were allotted as servants, although Jane Dundas became housekeeper to Phillip and, except for a period in England, remained in Government House until her death in 1805. Later, after the settlement at Rose Hill (Parramatta) was formed, some women acted as hutkeepers for groups of about sixteen men.

Generally, however, it was remarked that for much of the time the women were idle.

The first ship to arrive from England (in June 1790) was the *Lady Juliana* with an 'unnecessary and unprofitable' cargo of 222 females, but very little in the way of provisions for the colony. At this period of semi-starvation, as Collins wrote, they were only 'a burden to the settlement ... incapable of doing any exertion toward their own maintenance'. Poor Collins was no male chauvinist; he spoke no more than the truth, especially as he and Phillip had hoped that more skilled tradesmen and farmers would be amongst the first reinforcements. And Collins did note that in the difficult times the women 'shared largely of such little comforts as were to be procured'.

Birth, marriage and death

Phillip encouraged the convicts to marry, although not very successfully after it was found that marriage carried no special privileges. Some couples may not have married because they had wives or husbands in England, and Catholics were perhaps not prepared to be married by a Church of England parson. It was some years before there was a Catholic priest.

In the first five years of the colony there were about 250 births, but despite the primitive conditions only three women died in childbirth. Their babies also died within a few weeks as there were no wet-nurses and no substitutes for breast milk. Most of the mothers were unmarried, but in many cases there was a stable association with the father, so that something like a family life was possible. Some of these families were disturbed when seamen, and later marines or officials, had to return to England. Then the fathers had to make some provision for those they left behind. Some of the senior officials, such as surgeon White and P.G. King, took responsibility for the care and education of their children in England.

Sometimes long associations eventually led to marriage. Surgeon Arndell and Elizabeth Burley had the first of several children in 1790 and were married in 1807. Governor Macquarie, visiting the family, noticed the 'exemplary manner' in which the children were brought up.

A convict woman wrote home of the desperate and dreadful plight of the women, and it must certainly have been especially difficult for those left alone with a child. However, the great excess of males meant that many of these women married or formed other permanent relationships. That it was very much a man's world is shown by the sad case of Deborah Herbert. Married for only seven months, she accused her husband of beating her unjustly. She must have been a bad witness because the court ordered that she receive 25 lashes and return to him immediately!

The difficulties of 'keeping house' for the convict women were the same as for the marines' wives except that they probably had access to fewer little luxuries and fewer facilities, such as cooking utensils. Mary Phillips cleverly baked flour on an iron spade, for which she was given 25 lashes (spades were in short supply).

The women perhaps had less recreation than the men, but they did bathe in the sea and join in some of the parties.

A few of the women were able to return to England when their sentences had expired by undertaking some duties on board ships in return for their passage. Some began to establish shops and others conducted inns or lodging houses. But these developments were largely for later years.

The children

About 36 children arrived with the First Fleet, almost half of whom belonged to marine families. Two convicts, a boy and a girl, and six more young girls who arrived in 1790, all aged less than fifteen, were doubtless regarded as adults and led separate lives. We have no idea how these children were looked after or amused, except that their convict mothers were not compelled to work. There was no school in these years, and it is possible that the marine and convict children were not allowed to play together. The risks of play are shown by the drowning of two toddlers, one a marine's and the other a convict's child, in a sawpit and a claypit. Surprisingly, no child got lost in the bush and none is known to have got sunstroke, both common problems in later years. The open fires were another everyday hazard for young children.

There was widespread concern about the convict children because of their association with the uncouth and immoral convicts, making a good upbringing difficult or impossible. One little girl aged four was taken away from her mother, 'an abandoned character', who had been stabbed by the man she lived with and who had committed other crimes in the previous year. The child was sent, with an orphan convict child, to Norfolk Island. They were to be put in the care of a responsible person who was to receive extra land to cultivate for the children's benefit. They were also to be taught reading, writing and husbandry. The settlement on Norfolk Island was smaller, probably more orderly, and food supplies at that period were slightly more reliable. It is likely that two or three other children were sent away from Sydney for similar reasons.

Whatever criticisms were levelled at the women, they were not transferred to the children. They were described as 'fine, healthy, strong children as ever were seen', a fact attributed to the climate. Certainly the sunshine would have acted to prevent rickets. This disorder, then common in England, produces bone deformities due to lack of vitamin D which sunlight helps to avoid. One convict differed: he thought the poor quality of the salt meat made many of the children unhealthy. He was probably speaking of infants, and here there must have been a difficulty. How to wean a baby, when there is no milk, no feeding cups or bottles and only flour, salt pork, sweet corn, poor rice and probably worse water? Probably the mothers breast-fed their babies for a year or more if possible. Perhaps also they boiled some cereal into a pap, maybe with some of the 'soup' from boiled salt meat, wrapped the mess in a piece of rag, tied the ends and gave it to the child to suck. Weaning is teething time, and we know from Norfolk Island records that infants died of 'teething'. The true cause would have been a severe form of infant diarrhoea and vomiting. This is not surprising with the lack of knowledge about germs and hygiene at that period. The condition was more likely to occur in summer, perhaps because of the greater number of flies and the shorter time for which food could be kept before 'going off'. It remained a serious risk for young children in Australia for over a hundred years.

The ration scale for children was mentioned in Chapter 1. Phillip recognised the special needs of growing children and did not reduce their rations during the hungry years. Collins mentioned that many of the children could have eaten part of their mothers' rations as well as their own. The children were hungry, like everyone else, but they nearly all survived these years.

We do have some facts on births and deaths. There were about 250 babies born in the first five years of the settlement and nearly 80 deaths in childhood. Two-thirds of these deaths occurred in children less than three years old, that is, at the susceptible 'teething' age. Most of the deaths happened in two epidemics at the beginning and end of the period. In between, the death rate for the children was remarkably low, about a third of what would have been expected in England at that period. Nowadays, of course, we would not expect even two or three of these children to die. The birth rate is a little below the average for those times, possibly because the poor food supply did not help the women to bear children.

The reasonably high birth rate and the low death rate meant that the number of children in the settlement grew rapidly. There were five women for every child in 1788 but within ten years or so there was one child for every woman, and most of the children were less than seven or eight years of age. This gave rise to the impression that the Sydney climate made women particularly fertile, that is, more likely to have children, than in England.

All the figures show that somehow the women must have managed to look after their children very well, despite the difficulties. Indeed, the very few childhood deaths between the two epidemics (which also affected the adults) suggest that they learned from the experience of just one year of living in the camp conditions of the first settlement. The one circumstance which did help them was that the dangerous infectious diseases, such as measles, diphtheria and whooping cough, did not survive the long voyage to Australia. These and some other diseases were absent from the colony for almost half a century.

One can only guess what all those children did to amuse themselves all day. But remember that in those days a child of seven or eight was expected to do the best part of a day's work, perhaps in the gardens or looking after the fowls and even the pigs. After all, Major Ross's son, John, was appointed a second-lieutenant in the marines at the age of nine, although it is doubtful whether he did any serious duty! The children rapidly grew to be taller than their parents, who were very short by our standards (the men averaged about 166 cm and the women were about 10 cm shorter). They tended to be slender, wiry and fair-haired, so they came to be called Cornstalks. Every observer in later years praised their good behaviour, despite their convict origins.

The Aborigines

Governor Phillip's instructions from the British government regarding the natives he would certainly meet were definite but not detailed. They were to be treated with friendliness and respect, so that both Europeans and Aborigines might exist together in peace. There was to be no 'unnecessary interruption' of their 'usual occupations'. No one realised that simply by occupying their land and fishing in their harbour, the newcomers automatically upset the Aborigines' normal occupation of food gathering in their tribal area. Phillip extended his instructions to the convicts and his staff by stressing that the Aborigines were not to be harmed, and certainly not to be shot at.

An important factor in the attitude of Phillip and his officers to the Aborigines was the enormous interest amongst scientists, and indeed all learned men, in 'the noble savage'. They thought that perhaps the simple life of 'uncivilised' natives was really happier and more satisfying than the complicated life of 'civilised' peoples; perhaps native races had inherited the Garden of Eden. This concern gave Europeans a special interest in the customs, religion, way of life and language of the native people all over the world.

Phillip and his officers were well aware of this interest, and some of them made special efforts to find out and record all they could, knowing the information would bring them credit amongst the wise men at home. Thus, John White's book describes and illustrates Aboriginal implements, including a fish hook and basket, as well as spears. David Collins devoted many pages to Aboriginal customs and was one of several officers to list a

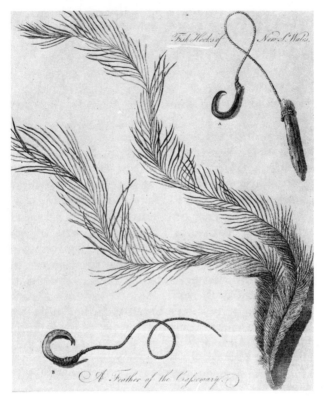

Aboriginal fish hooks and an emu feather   John White

large number of Aboriginal words with their meanings; we know that Phillip himself, as well as King and Dawes, helped in this work. Almost all the journal writers wrote something of their observations on the Aborigines. Indeed, it is obvious that one or two of them, Collins in particular, must have gained the confidence and friendship of the Aboriginal people. In a way, the interest in the Aborigines may be seen as the same sort of curiosity which was shown to the unfamiliar native flora and fauna, which of course also interested people in England.

Early contact

The early contacts between the two races were

nervous but generally friendly on both sides. Each was curious about the other. If the Aborigines were astonished by the clothes and the white skins of the colonists, the Europeans were no less amazed by what seemed to them an extraordinarily primitive way of life and a much less sophisticated society than Captain Cook had described in the South Sea Islands and New Zealand.

For months Phillip was frustrated in trying to learn more about the Aborigines because they withdrew from the area of the camp when they realised the visitors were apparently going to stay indefinitely. Contacts became intermittent, brief and more or less unpredictable. Furthermore, probably because of thoughtless acts of the convicts, such as stealing Aboriginal belongings to trade with the seamen returning home, the relationship between the two races began to deteriorate, as shown by some incidents already mentioned in this book. Once only did Phillip lose his temper and retaliate. After one of his servants had died as a result of a spear wound in the chest (the man was known to have annoyed and even shot at the Aborigines), he proposed to send out a patrol to kill several natives at random as a reprisal. This provoked some disagreement with his officers, especially Dawes, but fortunately the patrol found no Aborigines to kill. One can scarcely imagine that a troop of marines marching through the bush would surprise any Aboriginal group, especially if the officer in charge had little heart for the job.

Many incidents reveal the lack of understanding which each race had for the other. Presents of fish, axes and trinkets produced temporary harmony on several occasions, but the Europeans did not realise that these were not regarded as generous gifts but simply as a perfectly natural, unremarkable, sharing of food and possessions; this was the Aboriginal way. Nor could the Aborigines understand that when they wanted to 'borrow' any European belongings they were often refused; to the European, this was pilfering or downright theft.

Two drawings of Aborigines from D. Collins' *Account of the Colony in New South Wales* 1798 showing preliminary initiation ceremonies for boys

The white people could not reconcile the Aborigines' obvious distress at seeing a man flogged with their own apparent enjoyment of fights and especially their apparent cruelty to their own womenfolk.

Some incidents had their amusing side. Both parties laughed when an unsuspecting Aborigine put his hand in a kettle of boiling water to take out a fish which was being cooked. Lieutenant Bradley tells of the surgeon shooting a crow and waving it at some Aborigines in canoes as an invitation to them to land. Finding that they were too shy or frightened to do so, the surgeon threw the bird towards them. But the bird had only been stunned; it had recovered and promptly flew away. 'This remarkable event appeared to them as though [we had] power to give and take life [and it] astonished them so much, that they remained quite silent some time & then all joined in a loud exclamation of wonder.'

On another occasion surgeon Worgan was about to shoot a crow when a very distressed Aborigine ran up and put his hand over the muzzle of the gun, obviously pleading for the crow's life. Worgan 'complied with his Request, and laughed off the Offence I had seemingly given, at which he seemed mightily pleased'. He understood that the crow meant something special to that man but he could not possibly understand the reason. We may guess that the bird had some totem or religious significance. Similarly, but much more seriously, the visitors could not possibly understand the Aborigines' special attitude to the land they had occupied, nor could they know of the religious beliefs that gave special importance to sacred sites which were unwittingly desecrated.

Kidnap and disease

Phillip's inability to learn about the Aborigines while they remained so distant eventually led him to arrange to kidnap one in December 1788.

Manly, or Arabanoo, as he was called, was first confined to the settlement by roping him to a convict. He adapted himself quite quickly to European clothing and habits; he ate the food and preferred tea to wine. He even began to look quite contented with his lot. He dined at the governor's table, and on 9 May 1789 he had dinner with Captain Hunter and others on board the *Sirius*, just back from its voyage around the world for supplies. Little more than a week later he was dead of the smallpox.

It was about a month earlier that this dreadful disease had appeared amongst the Aborigines. The first the settlers knew of it was the discovery of many dead bodies. A family of sick and dying were found and a man and his young son brought in to the settlement; a little later a girl and her brother were also brought in. Arabanoo helped to nurse them and to bury those who died, and in the course of this he obviously caught the infection. The epidemic is discussed in a little detail in the Appendix. A boy, Nanbarray, aged about ten, and a girl, Abaroo, about thirteen, survived. Nanbarray was then adopted by surgeon White, and the girl went to live with the Reverend Johnson and his wife. These two orphan children played no small part in bridging the gap between the two cultures. They acted as interpreters, probably not only in relation to language but also to customs. Nanbarray had a long and interesting association with the settlement but Abaroo eventually returned to her own people.

But the children, whose tribe had virtually disappeared as a result of the smallpox, could not provide all the information Phillip wished to obtain. After the disappointment of losing Arabanoo probably just when he was becoming helpful, Phillip decided to try to kidnap two more men. Bradley found this 'by far the most unpleasant service I ever was ordered to Execute'. His two captives were Colbee, who soon escaped but who was eventually to develop a close association with the settlement, and Bennelong. Bennelong did not escape for six months, during which time he acquired all the European ways (the Aborigines were marvellous mimics). He learned a good deal of English and was a very popular figure in the settlement. He became very attached to Governor Phillip and later returned voluntarily to the settlement. Eventually he accompanied the governor to England. After his return he is said to have lived in a hut on what is now Bennelong Point where the Sydney Opera House is now located.

By 1791 Collins, the Reverend Johnson, Tench (whose discussion of the Aborigines is very readable and very sympathetic) and even Sergeant Scott, were writing of the more frequent visits of the Aborigines to the settlement. By this time the smallpox epidemic had greatly reduced their number and disorganised their tribal organisation. Perhaps with that awful disease and death they had lost some of their independence and some of their cultural strength and cohesion.

Collins in fact was pleased that 'the friendly intercourse with the natives which had been so earnestly desired was at length established', and 'by slow degrees we began mutually to be pleased with, and to understand each other'. This is an encouraging note on which to end this chapter but in fact Collins was recording the first signs of the submission of Aboriginal to European culture. The rapport was not to last, and the Aborigines were to find that in fact it threatened both their identity and their existence.

It was the beginning of a process inevitably repeated countless times in the evolution of civilisation (as we know it) since its beginnings thousands of years ago. In a conflict of cultures one must win; one can only hope to minimise the losses of the other. Two centuries later, with a little more understanding and the wisdom of a little hindsight, some effort is being made to retrieve and preserve a unique culture which was almost lost for ever.

Epilogue

At the start I outlined the background to the first settlement and its early problems. In subsequent chapters we have looked at how the members of the several classes spent their time. To keep all this in perspective, we should briefly review the major events, problems and achievements of Governor Phillip's administration.

There were certainly mistakes in the arrangements for the first Australian colony. Stores, including clothing, medicines and ammunition, were left behind; some of the provisions were inferior; and the tools and equipment were insufficient and of poor quality. There were no skilled overseers for the convicts, and too few of the convicts themselves were tradesmen or experienced in farming.

There were also miscalculations. Largely because of descriptions given by Captain Cook and Sir Joseph Banks, Botany Bay was thought to be more fertile and more suitable for the speedy development of a self-sufficient colony than in fact the whole area east of the Blue Mountains proved to be. It was not foreseen that the marines would not supervise the work of the convicts, and the unsuitability of the timber for housing construction was also unexpected.

Finally, there were unpredictable misfortunes. Most of the sheep which survived the voyage were killed in a thunderstorm, and the cattle were lost. There was no fodder for the few horses, which were not suitable for the country at this stage; they were not used (except perhaps for food). For various reasons, chiefly the unreliable rainfall and poor cultivation techniques, the crops failed and drought threatened the water supply. The wreck of the *Sirius* at the dangerous landing place on Norfolk Island precipitated a crisis, for the little *Supply* was then the only remaining link with the outside world, and further provisions were essential.

In 1790 a ship at last arrived from England, bringing women and welcome letters but few supplies. It was followed by the Second Fleet in which the convicts were scandalously and cruelly mismanaged, largely because of a system of payment per convict on embarkation rather than disembarkation. It made no difference to the contractor's fees if he delivered them dead or alive. Many did die (over 25 per cent) and those who landed were almost all sick, many more dying after their arrival. It was only another burden for the struggling settlement to bear. In 1792 the Third Fleet arrived, not quite so unhealthy, but destined to suffer an alarming number of deaths in the next few months. The size of this epidemic was frightening, with convicts dying at the rate of nearly a hundred each month for reasons which are not definitely known. Probably the basis was poor morale amongst these new arrivals: in the face of hardship and disease they lost the will to live. The marine battalion was withdrawn, and the colony got the doubtful benefit of the New South Wales Corps instead.

The greatest misfortune of all was the wreck of HMS *Guardian* on an iceberg off the Cape of Good Hope in 1789. The ship was carrying essential supplies and personnel, specially selected in England to relieve many of the worries and problems set out in Phillip's first despatches home. Had it arrived safely in the colony it is reasonable to believe that the colony's hardships would have been less and progress towards self-sufficiency made faster.

Throughout the hungry years, Phillip never lost faith in the future of the settlement; he regarded all his problems as temporary. Not all his officers, and probably very few of the convicts, had the same confidence. There is little doubt that by organising the rations as he did he saved the lives of the whole community. He could not have given the convicts any less and expect them to survive. If he had given the marines more, as he was pressed to do, the provisions would have been used up before any further stores could have arrived. As it was, Collins said that were it not for the deaths, and the consequent saving in rations, all might have starved.

Phillip's leadership, courage and confidence must have been something of an inspiration, even if people sometimes grumbled about him. The best evidence for this is that the survival rate of the First Fleet convicts was astonishingly good, despite all the difficulties. Only about 11 per cent of them died over five years, and this was far from the experience of later arrivals (15 per cent of the Third Fleet convicts died in their first year in the colony). Somehow, Phillip gave his people the will to live, or at least those whom he had time enough

Governor Phillip

to influence. The marines and officers lost a small proportion of their numbers, doubtless reflecting their slightly better standard of living over the years.

In the last year or so Phillip had been periodically ill, particularly with a recurring pain in his side. He had received permission to take leave in England but planned to delay this for a little time. Suddenly, he changed his mind and left on the next ship, the *Atlantic*, in December 1792. Perhaps he was mentally and physically exhausted after five years of arduous, unremitting and lonely responsibility and perhaps also he could see that Major Grose, in command of the New South Wales Corps, would be at least as difficult to work with as Ross had been.

Phillip's departure was the end of an era. Scarcely was his ship beyond the harbour before Major Grose, who had been nine months in the colony, introduced radical changes in his predecessor's policies. He gave the soldiers better rations than the convicts, and he substituted virtually military rule for the magistrate's courts. He allowed the officers and other privileged persons an almost complete monopoly on trade (which Phillip had discouraged), he gave them land grants and convicts to work them. In so doing, he probably paved the way for more rapid economic and agricultural development but perhaps he also sowed the seeds of the famous Bligh rebellion. But all this lay in the future, a future which was possible as the result of the work of one man — and his convicts.

Appendix: the smallpox epidemic

The origin of the terrifying epidemic which killed probably hundreds of Aborigines in 1789 has not been definitely identified. It did not arise directly from the British settlement or the visiting French fleet because neither had experienced any cases of this disease. Once patients have fully recovered from smallpox, which may take six weeks, they are no longer infectious. The most plausible explanation is that it was introduced by traders from islands to the north of Australia and that it then swept right down the east coast.

Another possibility, which has had some recent publicity, is that the epidemic arose from 'variolous matter' brought out in bottles by the surgeons on the First Fleet. This needs some explanation. 'Variolous matter' was obtained from the 'blisters' which develop during smallpox, which has a rash similar to chicken pox. Either the fluid was taken from the blister, or the crust from a broken blister was collected. Both would contain the living virus of genuine smallpox. Introduced into the skin of a person (usually a child) who had never had smallpox, it would cause a mild attack of smallpox — hopefully, and usually, this was the case, but it could also cause a fatal or severe attack. If the patient recovered he or she would be immune to the disease in the future. Of course, as the material caused real smallpox, this practice of 'inoculation' or 'variolation' could effectively start an epidemic of its own, and in an epidemic up to 20 per cent of the sufferers might die. These dangers were recognised, and variolation was falling into disfavour in Britain by the late decades of the eighteenth century. Nonetheless, it was an understandable approach at that time towards reducing the effects of a common and often fatal disease.

Knowing the risks, the First Fleet surgeons would have been very reluctant to use the 'variolous matter' except in exceptional circumstances. If smallpox had appeared on the voyage out or in the early settlement, they might have inoculated the susceptible young children, that is, those who had not had smallpox, but no such problem arose. Most of the adults would have had smallpox already, and would be immune. It was not difficult to know who had had smallpox because it often left scars, or pock marks, especially on the face (some years later over 20 per cent of child convicts had pock marks). The surgeons were in fact impressed by the absence of all the common infectious diseases of Europe, and there is no way they would have wished, for the safety of the whole population, to start one going. It is also impossible to believe that the use of the 'variolous material' would have gone unrecorded by someone, particularly as antagonism to its use was common in England. Finally, it is unlikely that the virus would have survived two years and the voyage to Australia, although this is just possible if crusts were used. Modern studies suggest that the virus would usually not survive more than a few months.

Overall, it is more probable that the bottles were lost, discarded or reused for more practical purposes than that their contents were put into the skin of any colonial child. In support of this is the fact that there is no suggestion of using the material when a legitimate emergency did arise, that is, when the Aboriginal epidemic occurred. If the 'variolous matter' were still about, this might have been the occasion to take the known risks, and at least to consider the possibility of inoculating the colonial-born children. There is no hint of this amongst the several recorders of the settlement's activities. Tench, the only person to note the previous existence of the 'matter', does not even mention the possibility, as he would surely have done if it were still available.

One historian has suggested that the surgeons may have deliberately inoculated the Aborigines, perhaps with the intent of contributing to their extermination. It is difficult to see any reasonable basis for this view. It would have been flatly contrary to Phillip's London instructions and his own instructions to his staff. It would be contrary to the humanitarian views expressed and demonstrated by the governor and his colleagues on other occasions. Had the surgeons done so, the fear of smallpox among the Europeans themselves would have made it impossible for them to take some of the sick Aborigines into the camp. That they did so, at a significant (and known) risk to themselves, and especially to their children, argues strongly against their starting the epidemic; that they would have taken the extra risk of killing their own kind as well is unbelievable. As it was, only one negro convict caught the disease even though the children were, surprisingly, allowed some contact with the sick. Perhaps this occurred before it was realised that the Aborigines had smallpox, or more likely Arabanoo had become their friend.

At a more practical level, it is doubtful if the surgeons would have had the opportunity to carry out inoculation; contact with the Aborigines in this period was episodic and brief. To have done so secretly is even more implausible, especially as White and Balmain, none too friendly to one another, would have been unlikely to collaborate. If Arabanoo had been kidnapped for this very purpose, and if the surgeons were interested to experiment, then he was the obvious choice. However, the epidemic was observed only after his capture, and a month before his death. He undoubtedly caught the disease from the family that were brought into the hospital after they had been found by Sergent Scott and his party on 15 April 1789. Arabanoo did not fall ill until towards the middle of May.

One might ask whether, two centuries later, it matters what caused this epidemic. Of course it does, especially if it was promoted deliberately, if we are to understand the significance of the historical fact. I have discussed the question in some detail to indicate that the historian has a responsibility not only to record events but also to try to understand, or work out, how and why they occurred. And of course, at the time of an epidemic, it is even more important for doctors and health officials to understand quickly exactly how and why the epidemic arose and how it is spreading. In this way they can often take steps to control the situation. A final answer on that tragic smallpox epidemic is perhaps unlikely to be found but we have at least examined the possibilities.